The Language of Life and Business Coaching:

Advanced Skills That Will Help Your Clients Flourish

by Chad W. Hall, MCC

Published by Coach Approach Ministries
2425 North Center Street #236, Hickory, NC 28601
coachapproachministries.org

ABOUT THE AUTHOR

Chad Hall is a Master Certified Coach who serves as Founder and President of Coach Approach Ministries, a non-profit organization that provides coaching and coach training services to Christian churches and leaders.

When he's not training coaches, you can find Chad working with church and business leaders and writing. Chad is the author of *Coaching for Christians Leaders: A Practical Guide* (2007) and *Faith Coaching: A Conversational Approach to Helping Others Move Forward in Faith* (2009), both of which are cornerstone texts in the field of Christian coaching. His 2015 eBook *The Coaching Mindset: 8 Ways to Think Like a Coach* has spent over 100 weeks as an Amazon Bestseller in three categories. His second eBook *Coach the Person, Not the Problem* (2016) has also been a longtime Amazon bestseller. He's the editor of *Christian Coaching Magazine* and has also written for *Leadership Journal* on a variety of issues.

Chad is a graduate of Lenoir-Rhyne College (BA in Religion), Duke Divinity School (MTS) and Princeton Theological Seminary (ThM). He also earned his Doctor of Ministry at Western Seminary with a research focus on Christian integration of positive psychology. Over his career Chad has served as a pastor, church planter and denominational consultant. He's also worked as an internal coach at technology leader SAS (Cary, NC).

Chad lives in Hickory, NC with his wife Holly and their three growing children. For fun he enjoys his children's sporting activities, restoring his '88 Jeep Grand Wagoneer, roasting his own coffee beans, and hiking the beautiful landscape of the Appalachian Mountains.

TABLE OF CONTENTS

INTRO: THE POWER OF COACHING

This book explores coaching as a language, akin to any other language such as Farsi or Japanese. While coaching is not a new branch on the tree of languages, it is a distinct way of speaking, no matter the language you speak. If you fail to recognize the distinct nature of coaching, you'll likely think learning to coach should be easy, and this misconception will prevent you from becoming a very good coach.

But before considering coaching as a language, let's ask an important question: why bother? Why take the time to learn or become fluent in the language of coaching? My answer is simple: by learning to speak the language of coaching, you open up the possibility of transforming lives through the words you speak and the words you help others speak. Case in point: Winston.

Winston served as the owner of a fast-growing and successful advertising firm. You probably know people like Winston. He's not just smart – he's sharp. A bit on the intense side, he can make the not-so-intense people who encounter him uncomfortable. He's okay making others uncomfortable since his main goal in life is to win. Yes, Winston is a winner — at least in the ways that most people measure things like that. Married to a lovely and faithful wife? Check. Plenty of social media pics showing his two kids enjoying time with dad while playing sports, skiing in the mountains of Utah, and serving the poor in some faraway place? Check. A man of character and charm who's also in great physical shape? Check, check, check. Before you start gagging or turning green with envy, let's skip the rest of the list. Rest assured that any other indicator of success you can think of deserves a big checkmark. We get the message: Winston is awesome.

So how could a guy like Winston possibly benefit from working with a coach?

I start this book with Winston's story to demonstrate the power of coaching. Winston wanted coaching because even the "winners" in life need support. Whatever vision of "the good life" or "success" or "contentment" you and I can conjure in our powerful brains, the people who've turned those visions into reality have not finished living. And so long as there is more life to be lived, even the most successful people benefit mightily from coaching.

Winston hired me to coach him a few years ago. Why? There were several factors, but it mostly came down to a recurring dream of his children as young adults. In reality, his kids were grade-school aged, but in the dream they were older and they were not happy. They were also not good. In fact, they were downright lazy. Winston was unsettled by what he saw in his dreams: children who took their wealth for granted, who lacked a desire to work or serve, and who seemed miserably lacking direction or motivation. Many clients hire a coach in order to turn a dream into reality; Winston hired me to avoid such a fate.

Over the next few months, Winston experienced deep change. At first the changes were on the surface: adjustments to his parenting style and his approach to long-term wealth. Over time he started to experience a transformation in how he saw the world, how he saw himself in the world, and the role he played in life. Eventually, he shifted away from trying to control and manage every aspect of life to make sure he won (however he might have defined a win). Finally, he admitted that while he was responsible for being the best parent he could be, he could not do anything to guarantee his children's future success, happiness, or goodness. While many of you already know this basic parenting truth, Winston did not. He needed the support of a coach to help him let go of an unrealistic set of assumptions concerning the people he loved the most.

I start this eBook with Winston's story because his experience illustrates well the power of coaching. Working with a coach can change a person's life for the better — but not if we coach poorly. If you are a coach who wants to make a positive difference in the lives of those you coach, then it behooves you to learn and master the language of coaching. In other words, don't just read this book; let it move you closer toward being the masterful coach that you can be (and that your clients need you to be).

Before we go any further, let me offer just a few quick reminders that will help you get the most from this book.

First, this book is not for beginners. If this is the first (or second or third) book you've read on coaching, you'll be better served to put it down, take a coaching class or two, practice coaching, and then come back to the book once you're more familiar with coaching. If you're not sure what coaching is, how it differs from counseling, mentoring, consulting, etc., what a coaching conversation sounds like, or what a coaching relationship entails, then most of this book will be unhelpful until you understand coaching better.

Second, basic coaching skills are powerful. Listening and asking questions are the real "meat and potatoes" of coaching, and with those skills you can promote new awareness and new action for those you coach. This book is not primarily about those basic skills, although this book will enhance those skills. This is not another book with lists of powerful questions or lessons on how to listen deeply. While those are wonderful things to know and practice, you'll be disappointed if you're looking for this book to provide quick tips or simple samples.

Third, this book is concerned with advanced coaching skills. By developing these advanced skills, you will engage each coaching conversation more naturally, create better rapport with your clients and generate greater results. But advanced skills don't come easily. It's not that hard to learn to walk a straight line (basic skill), but walking a tightrope (advanced skill) is in a whole different league. My advice is to read and understand Section One (Coaching as a Second Language) and then to move onto each of the language elements in Section Two, taking them one at a time. Rushing through the language elements is no way to develop advanced coaching proficiency, nor is simply reading the contents of this book. Go slowly and practice as you go. Read a chapter, try to implement what you learn, then revisit the chapter with your latest attempt fresh in your mind. Eventually you will master most of the language elements and before you know it, you'll be coaching at a masterful level. When that happens, your confidence will go way up as will your clients' satisfaction.

I hope you enjoy and benefit from this eBook. If you do, please leave a review at Amazon so other coaches can discover the book, benefit from your review, and gain fluency in speaking the language of coaching.

SECTION 1

Five Stages in Learning
the Language of Coaching

Coaching as a Second Language

I contend that learning to coach is a lot like learning to speak a new language. In order to become fluent in the language of coaching, one encounters many of the same challenges faced by someone attempting to develop the ability to speak a second language.

Like many American teenagers in the 1980s, I took Spanish during my junior and senior years of high school. I also took a few semesters of Spanish in college. I didn't try too hard in any of these classes, so I made B's en route to learning enough Spanish to carry on a 90-second conversation about what to have for lunch, the location of the bathroom, or the price of a sombrero. My fluency level did little to help me get around Guatemala during a two-week mission trip shortly after college graduation. Honestly, I'm not a language person. It's an understatement to say that new languages do not come easily to me.

Later in life, as a student at Duke Divinity School (where one trains to be a church leader), I took a class in New Testament Greek. Being a bit more focused in my mid-20's than I had been as a high school and college student, I was far more disciplined in learning the language. The class was graded on the curve, with only two students earning an A+ grade, and I was proud to earn my spot as one of those students. I aced the class but not the language. These days (twenty years later) my Greek skills are practically non-existent. When I see a college fraternity house, I'm lucky to get two of the three letters above the front door. While I was able to learn the language well enough to pass the quizzes and final exam, I never really absorbed the language in any meaningful way.

Why is learning a new language so difficult for me (and many others like me)? One of the primary reasons stems from the fact that I'm an American and I don't *have to* learn a new language. We English speakers are spoiled; we aren't forced or even expected to learn a second language. If I had lived in Guatemala for two years instead of visiting for two weeks, I would have needed to develop my Spanish ability in order to survive. Necessity drives fluency.

Learning a new language also proves challenging when your exposure comes mostly in the classroom versus being immersed in it. Speaking Spanish for an hour during class doesn't cut it. The same was true for Greek: had I gone on to become a pastor who used Greek on a weekly basis during sermon prep, I would have sharpened those skills. Instead, I got into leadership development, training, and eventually coaching. I wasn't immersed in Greek, so nearly all the ability I had worked so hard to develop went away. Becoming truly fluent in a new language is difficult enough that only the most motivated or naturally talented people can do it.

Okay, so what does all of this have to do with coaching? I am suggesting that learning to coach is a lot like learning to speak a new language. It's challenging. If you aren't coaching on a regular basis, it's almost impossible to become proficient. And if you aren't highly motivated to learn, then you'll most likely never develop beyond the basics. However, even if you are highly motivated and you are coaching regularly, learning to coach effectively still is no cakewalk.

Learning to coach is like acquiring a new language because coaching is an atypical way of holding conversations. Coaching conversations have a different pattern, a distinct flavor, and content unlike ordinary conversations. We may still be speaking English (or whatever our primary language may be) when we coach, but we are speaking this language with a new intent, employing new strategies, and with a new mindset.

While coaching is not a new branch on the tree of languages, it is a distinct way of speaking. If you fail to recognize the distinct nature of coaching, you'll likely think learning to coach should be much easier than it actually is, and this misconception will retard your development as a coach.

I don't mean to deter you. While learning to coach is far from easy, it is totally doable. And if I can learn to master this new language, so can you.

Learning your primary language was quick and easy, right? No, not so much. For the first year of life, you had no words — just grunts, groans, cries, and coos. Only after observing other people talk, talk, talk, did you take a chance and mutter your first word. And let's be honest, you were trying to say, "More smashed peas, please," but all they heard was, "Ma... ma...." The immediate adoration and celebration let you know that you'd succeeded in combining some sounds in a way that got results.

Learning a primary language is neither quick nor easy, but learning a second language is even more of a challenge. To help you learn coaching, let's consider the five stages of learning a language and how each stage applies to coaching.

Stage One

Silent and Receptive

The best way to start learning a new language is to listen. As you listen, you begin to notice the words that are used and the rules that determine how those words get used and arranged. You picked up on these rules of the language even before knowing what the rules were called or knowing that there was such a thing as rules. As you learned English, you picked up on the fact that the subject typically comes before the verb, and that an adjective usually precedes the noun it modifies.

Whoa! Wait a minute. Before you have an intense flashback to diagraming sentences in middle school, I promise we are not going to get into gerunds or dangling participles. The point here is simply that when you learned English, you did so by listening and recognizing that "The boy (subject) bounced (verb) the green (adjective) ball (noun)" instead of "The ball green boy bounced." One is a sentence with meaning and the other is gibberish.

If you learned a second language later in life, you applied the same first step, but with greater intentionality and with a conscious understanding of what a "rule" is when it comes to language. This same first step applies to coaching: you start by learning the basic rules of the language.

When you first learn to coach, the best way to start is by observing and learning how coaching works. Fortunately, you don't have to learn how to conjugate verbs, but you do need to know what coaching is, how it's distinct from other forms of conversing, and some of the basic rules, such as *asking* is better than *telling*.

You can learn about coaching from reading a book on coaching or by observing someone else coach, or even by being coached. While reading about coaching in a book — even an arguably brilliant book like this one! — will help you get started, you cannot master the language of coaching if you remain merely at this stage. So let's explore Stage Two.

Stage Two

Clunky Translating

When I was a kid, I decided to learn Latin by studying the mottos of various states. Surprisingly, this did not work. I wanted to say something profound like, "I love hamburgers" in Latin, but my approach was based on a faulty assumption that all I needed to do was replace the English word with the Latin word and then, presto! I would be able to speak Latin. Frustrated at my failure, I determined that it was no wonder Latin was a dead language: they had no word for *hamburger*. *Quod erat demonstrandum.*

As silly as my effort to learn Latin was, learning a second language requires something similar. Stage Two is the time when you try to translate what you already know in one language into the new language. This is the time for flash cards and vocabulary building. The same is true in coaching.

New coaches often try to use coaching techniques as a substitute for more directive techniques. At this stage, you're using the new and unfamiliar skills of coaching in an attempt to accomplish what you think should happen. If your native tongue is telling or fixing, you might attempt to make a clunky and incoherent translation aimed at telling people what to do, but now with questions. Instead of telling you son to clean his room, you might ask, "Don't you think it would be a good idea to clean your room?" This is not coaching — at least not yet.

I've trained hundreds of coaches, and I have seen many of them stall at this stage. They want to use the language of coaching to accomplish their own agenda. Often I'll hear Stage Two coaches proclaim, "Oh, coaching is about asking questions so the other person thinks it was their idea." They sometimes equate coaching to the Socratic method. In class, these coaches will confess, "I want to give advice, but I can't figure out how to do that as a coach." Others will proclaim, "I felt like my client didn't understand the situation properly, so I tried to ask questions that would help him see what was really going on." When you're trying to use coaching to tell, direct, and advise, you're in this stage of clunky translating.

Stage Three

Awkward but Effective

If you stick with a new language, you get to the stage where you can string a few sentences together and actually speak the language. The sentences are simple and they're probably not grammatically correct. It's all kind of awkward, but it gets the job done at a basic level. Two or three years of Spanish class in high school will get you to this level. You can communicate, but you really have to think about what you're doing, and speaking the new language takes a lot of effort because the language is still very foreign to you.

This is the stage I reached as a Spanish speaker. Now that my daughter is a high school Spanish student, she and I can converse in Spanish at a very basic level. Since we are far from fluent, we never carry on a serious conversation in Spanish. Neither of us has the ability to truly converse in Spanish, but we can carry on short, awkward conversations.

Coaches who reach this stage demonstrate traits of beginner coaches: they are capable of coaching, but it's not natural, it's not yet normal, and they often do it poorly. These coaches are very aware of the "rules" to coaching: ask open-ended questions, ask short questions, ask about outcomes, summarize and paraphrase, etc. This hyper-awareness of the rules can cause their coaching to be overly rigid and mechanical. On the other hand, even though these coaches are aware of the rules and try hard to coach correctly, they often break the rules without realizing it as they revert to their normal way of saying things when caught in a pinch. This stage of coaching can last months or even years.

Even in this novice state of competency, the coach still gets results. The coach is able to help the client focus, gain some new awareness, and commit to meaningful actions even though the coaching is not at a professional level and certainly is not "by the book." So even though such clumsy coaching may be like nails on a chalkboard to the people at the International Coach Federation, your clients will still receive value from the coaching you provide at this level.

Stage Four

Thinking Like a Coach

Those who speak a language long enough, practice hard enough, and really commit to it eventually reach the place where they not only speak the language but actually think in that language. These speakers have eliminated the lag that comes from thinking in one language and then mentally translating into the new language before speaking out loud. These are fluent speakers who can operate with ease and effectiveness when it comes to their "second" language.

A major stride in the development of any coach comes when he thinks like a coach instead of having to make him or herself translate non-coaching thoughts into coaching. Coaches who reach this level of fluency have changed the way they think, not just the way they speak. The results are powerful. This is professional-level coaching — the kind of coaching a client is more than willing to pay for because the results are so valuable.

When you think like a coach, you don't have to think about coaching because you've internalized the "rules" of coaching. In fact, instead of needing to intentionally coach, you can intentionally decide to bend or even break the rules when doing so will serve the client and the client's agenda. When you think like a coach, you can provide a few more insights because you know how to offer your insights in service to the client. You can share some of your own experience because you are able to do so in a way that keeps the focus on the client. And you can take many more risks because you're comfortable, confident, and willing to trust the coaching process more than you trust your ability to be the perfect coach.

Stage Five

Coaching with Beauty and Complexity

I'll never forget the day my high school Spanish teacher told our class that she dreams in Spanish. To really understand the impact of this news, you have to know that my teacher was perhaps the furthest thing from a native Spanish speaker that you can imagine. She was a slightly gray-haired older version of Marion Cunningham, the TV mom from the sitcom *Happy Days*. I'm sure if she ever had a DNA ancestry test it revealed zero percent Spanish or Latin American genes. So the realization that this milky white Southern woman had so immersed herself in the Spanish language and culture that she actually dreamed in Spanish simply amazed me and my classmates. She was beyond fluent; she could compose poetry, make inside jokes, and communicate in Spanish better than many native Spanish speakers.

Some coaches go beyond the professional level of fluency and effectiveness; they become so proficient that they can coach with beauty and complexity. Now to be clear, I'm not saying they make things complicated. Instead, they are capable of coaching very complex situations because they are capable of bringing the creativity and mastery that's needed by certain clients and certain coaching topics.

Not every coach will (or needs to) get to this level of fluency. I estimate that 95% of all coaching clients/topics are well-served by coaches with Stage Four ability. So what kind of coaching situation warrants Stage Five ability? Mostly it's when incredible creativity and resourcefulness from the coach is needed to tap into the client's creativity and resourcefulness.

Let's be clear: creativity for the sake of creativity is not helpful. Not even poets use poetry when ordering pizza. Stage Five coaches harness their coaching genius and tap into their creativity only when appropriate. For example, if a client needs to come up with options for addressing a challenging situation, the Stage Five coach might use a pretty straightforward (Stage Four) technique such as brainstorming or best/worst contrasting to get the client's thinking unstuck. But if such a technique proved less than powerful, the Stage Five coach might come up with a creative technique right there on the spot. This never-before-tried technique would be based on the coach's deep well of knowledge, ability, and coaching fluency as well as what was happening in that moment with that client.

In the same way that a novelist or poet knows all the rules of language and grammar, but might choose to bend, break, or re-imagine those rules, the Stage Five coach knows all the "rules" and best practices of coaching but freely decides to bend, break, or re-imagine those rules. For example, a coach would never insult a client. That's bad humanity, not just bad coaching. But a Stage Five coach might use an insult to unlock a hidden motivation or to generate a powerful insight for the client. The "insult" is not really an insult, and the masterful coach would obviously have to believe this technique fits the moment, but the point is that the Stage Five coach is willing to take a creative risk in service to the client and is capable of leveraging such a technique. While a less-creative coach might be uneasy employing an "insult," the Stage Five coach does so confidently and with success.

SECTION 2

Five Shifts That Promote Fluency

Becoming a fluent, effective coach takes time and effort. And perhaps the most challenging aspect of becoming a great coach has to do with shifts in how you approach conversations. What you think should happen in a conversation pretty much determines your approach to the conversation, which in turn determines what you do in the conversation. So speaking the language of coaching isn't about learning the right words and then using those words — it's more about transitioning your approach. Following are five of the most crucial shifts you'll need to make in order to speak the language of coaching.

Shift One

Speak with Intentionality

Coaching is a type of conversation. Whether we're talking about coaching or any other type of conversation, it helps to know that every conversation has three components:

- Purpose: the reason for having the conversation.
- Process: the way the conversation unfolds and the structure that supports the purpose.
- Content: the actual substance of the conversation; what is said.

Conversations can be mapped according to two factors: intentionality and the extent to which that intentionality is made explicit. Conversations that are high in intentionality have a clear and strong purpose. Sometimes one conversation participant has a different intention than his or her partner, which can cause a problem. Conversations that are low in intentionality have no clear or compelling purpose — they are free to wander and change directions depending on what comes up in the conversation. Meanwhile, explicitness is the degree to which the conversation's intention (or lack of intention) is made obvious (explicit) between the parties to the conversation.

Implied Intentional. Some human conversations are implicitly intentional. That is, at least one of the parties has a very clear purpose for participating in the conversation, but that purpose needn't be shared out loud with the con-

	Implicit	Explicit
Intentional	Conversations that have a purpose, but the purpose is assumed and/or not clearly stated. Sometimes the purpose is known only to one party in the conversation. Examples: calling your parent to ask for money or talking with a salesperson.	Conversations for which there is a purpose and the reason for holding the conversation is clarified and agreed upon by both parties. Examples: a good business/team meeting or a called family meeting.
Unintentional	Conversations that are free to wander to various topics, focus on one thing, then move to another, and conclude whenever one or both parties choose to withdraw from the conversation. Examples: chatting with a friend over coffee or catching up with a family member on the phone.	Conversations where it is made obvious that there is no agenda and the conversations is free to wander from topic to topic. Examples: calling your parent, who asks why you called (thinking you wanted money) and you respond by letting them know you just wanted to chat.

versation partner because the implicit intentionality is obvious. For example, when you buy groceries, the implicit purpose for the interaction between customer and clerk is so strong that it need not be made explicit. After all, it would be kind of weird if you looked at the checkout clerk and said, "I would like to interact with you only for the purpose of knowing the cost of my items so that I may pay my amount and be on my way," to which the clerk responded, "Yes, and I would add that we engage in just enough small talk to remind me that I am human." Conversations that are routine and/or occur within a purpose-filled context tend to fall into this quadrant.

Implied Unintentional. Other conversations have no clear purpose and this fact is not made explicit by the parties to the conversation. Small talk between neighbors, coffee conversation between good friends, and daily dialogue between husband and wife falls into this quadrant. These conversations are free to roam from this to that and to fill however much time the two (or more) people wish to give. If one of the persons was to ask, "What would you like to talk about?" the other person would reply, "Nothing, I just want to talk with you." The purpose for the conversation is to connect and share, but beyond that there's no intended goal.

Explicit Unintentional. Once in a while you need to have an unintentional conversation and you need to make explicit that there is no greater purpose or agenda. I once had a manager with whom I'd have weekly one-on-one meetings. Usually we had a topic to discuss and we kept the meetings aimed at clear business matters. But once in a while neither of us had topics to discuss. When that happened, we'd often cancel the meeting, but other times she'd suggest we still meet and just talk. These conversations had no clear purpose and no intended destination, and we made this fact clear at the beginning of the conversation so that neither of us was confused about why we were meeting. Otherwise, one (or both) of us might assume there was an implied intention, which could cause some serious confusion.

Explicit Intentional. Finally, some of the best conversations are those that have a clear purpose, and for which the purpose is made obvious between the conversation participants. Rumor has it that sometimes a wife will share with her husband about how her mother is driving her crazy, and the husband goes into problem-solving mode when the wife really just wants to vent. Again, I have not experienced this firsthand, but I've heard tales of such occurrences. Such interactions would be improved if the intention for the conversation were made explicit since the wife's intention (vent) is not the same as the husband's (problem solve). Good business meetings are also explicit and intentional. There is a shared purpose for the meeting so that everyone is on the same page and everyone can help ensure the meeting moves in the right direction and toward the common goal.

Coaching conversations need to be explicit and intentional. The intention is to support the person being coached in clarifying a goal, discovering what's needed to reach that goal, and designing actions that will close the gap between the current reality and the goal. In formal coaching relationships this intent is clear because there is a written contract or agreement and both parties are "signing off" on this purpose. However, even though the intention for the coaching is explicit (contract), many coaches still wrestle with being intentional in the conversation. They mistakenly think that purposeful conversations are somehow bad. Instead of asking, "What do you want to focus on today?" these coaches chit-chat with their client in hopes that a coachable topic emerges. It won't.

To learn the language of coaching requires a shift to intentionality. Let's be clear, this shift does not have to come at the cost of kindness, empathy, or connection. The best coaches are incredibly intentional *and* very easy to talk with. They keep the conversation moving in the right direction with a style that is friendly, casual and inviting.

Shift Two

Keep the Conversation Spotlight Rightly Focused

Many conversations are like a game of ping-pong. These conversations have a back-and-forth nature to them: one person talks, then the other person talks, and so forth. This is a good thing. The back-and-forth rhythm keeps the conversation balanced and allows both parties to share and receive. Most of the normal conversations that you and I have with other human beings should be balanced, not one-sided. In fact, having a one-sided conversation is rather rude.

However, not all human conversations follow this norm. A sermon at church is one-sided. So is a political speech. A good radio or podcast interview is more one-sided in that the interviewer gives more room for the interviewee to talk. A mentoring relationship tends to expect the mentor to do most of the talking/sharing. When the conversation is not ideally balanced, there is a shared expectation of this fact. Otherwise, things get weird.

Coaching is another relationship in which the conversation dynamic should not be a back-and-forth rhythm. Instead of seeking balance and equal sharing/receiving, we shift to what might be considered a spotlight conversation. The focus of the conversation is primarily on one of the conversation partners (the client), and both parties know this, support this, and participate accordingly. What's really unusual about coaching is that the one doing most of the talking is also the one getting most of the benefit.

This is a major shift. Many new coaches struggle to make enough space for the person being coached to talk. These novice coaches are used to helping others by sharing, so they mistakenly think that if they aren't talking then they aren't helping. Nothing could be further from the truth. The best way to support the person being coached is to talk just enough (and in just the right ways) that the person being coached speaks more and their speech and thoughts get them somewhere new.

Coaches keep the spotlight shining on the client so the power of the conversation is leveraged for the client's benefit. However, we need to recognize that the spotlight can get hot. When all the attention of the conversation is on you, you're on the spot. You have to work. It's up to you to make the conversation productive and forward-moving. This new language dynamic can be challenging for both the coach and the person being coached. The coach has to be willing to keep the spotlight on the client even when – especially when – she is struggling. The coach cannot bail her out just because things get hard. Usually it's when things get challenging for the client that the best value comes to her.

So how do coaches keep the spotlight on the client? Of course, we shut up. That's obvious. The Clients cannot talk if we are talking. But being quiet is not enough. Clients need a true conversation partner, so we have to use both silence and speaking to keep the spotlight on them. Here are some of the ways our words keep the spotlight shining brightly on our clients:

- We ask powerful, probing, thought-provoking questions. When a client shares, our questions should invite him to share even more. We can't get into all the best practices for good coaching questions here, but just know that question are one of the primary tools we use.
- We practice active listening. When someone else is speaking, there are things you can do to let them know you are listening, you care what they are saying, and you are taking it all in. These signals indicate to the other person that they can keep talking. Some coaches use little phrases such as "Yeah," "Um hm," and "That's interesting," to indicate to the client that they are tracking and the client's words are being received by the coach. Summarizing and paraphrasing are lengthier ways we can use active listening to keep the spotlight on the client.

- We share, but always with a purpose. Letting the client do most of the talking is a good thing, but there can be too much of a good thing. If your client is talking 95% of the time, then you're probably not being very effective as a coach. The coach sometimes needs to share some things about the coach in order to serve the client. Sometimes it's as simple as a responding to the client's struggle with, "Me too!" Other times, you should share a short story about yourself, a truth you picked up from a book, or a piece of witty banter in response to what the client has shared. The key with any of these forms of sharing is to keep it concise, keep it relevant, and to always transition away from yourself and to the client. For example, if your client shares about last week's team meeting that went terribly wrong, you might respond with something along the lines of, "Wow, that sounds brutal. I remember once walking out of a team meeting thinking *That was as close to hell on earth as anything I ever want to experience.* In three words, what made your meeting so hellish?" That type of sharing can encourage ("You're not alone") and keep the spotlight on the client by inviting them to use your experience to explore their own experience more deeply. Beware that sharing too much or not effectively turning the conversation back to the client can derail the conversation.

Shift Three

Stop Sharing and Start Inviting

dmit it, sometimes your conversation partner (a coaching client, your spouse, or someone at work) is talking and you are pretending to listen, but you're really listening to yourself as you prepare your response to what they are saying. That's a no-no, but it's one we all do. Even if it's at a deeply subconscious level, we think, *As soon as you stop talking or give me some kind of doorway to respond, I'm going to share. And I can't wait to share!*

Coaches should shift away (way, way away) from this tendency. Instead of waiting to share, we invite the other person to share... at least the *good* coaches make this shift. The *not-so-good-yet* coaches formulate their "powerful" questions while the client is talking. They try to connect what the client is saying with what they already know or have experienced. They also prime their responses so they can slide them in as soon as they get a chance. This is bad coaching. Good coaches aren't waiting to talk; they are curious about the client and eager to hear the client talk. This is why good coaches invite the client to share.

This shift is simple to describe but hard to achieve. Why? Because we humans like to think, and we like to think about what we are thinking. We're always evaluating what others share and formulating opinions and responses that will reveal what we think. So how can we make this shift? The answer is to stop thinking. At least stop thinking so much.

The truth is that being "too smart" as a coach can be a real problem. This is why I often encourage my coaching students to "take a dumb pill." Stop trying to be so smart. Stop trying to solve the client's challenge. Stop trying to figure it all out. Stop trying to connect the client's challenge to your own experience or a book you read or a class you took or an insight you're having. But the truth is that it's hard to stop those seemingly smart activities.

It's hard to stop being smart (and waiting to share our brilliance) in some part because our brains are incredible pattern-matching machines. Your brain has evolved to connect new things to known things. When you see or hear something new, your brain wants to connect it to something familiar, something you've already encountered, something for which you have a category and maybe even a solution. But your awesome pattern-matching ability is not to your client's advantage because her brain is also an awesome pattern-matching machine and your job is to get her brain working, not show off how well yours works.

In order to stop your brilliant brain from getting in the way, try starting something else. After all, it's easier to break a bad habit if you can replace it with a good habit instead of just trying to eliminate the bad habit. I'd encourage you to replace your eagerness to share with a deep curiosity. Instead of waiting to add your two cents, practice drawing out the five, ten, or twenty-five cents the client has to share. It takes a lot of brilliance to remain curious and to draw out the best from a client, so being curious puts your brain to work on behalf of your client.

Shift Four

Provide Challenge More Than Comfort

To be fluent in the language of coaching, you also will have to make a fourth shift: from trying to keep others comforted in the conversation to challenging them effectively. Most of us think that supporting someone means helping ease their discomfort. If a friend is facing a tough situation, we're likely to offer something along the lines of, "Oh, I'm sure it will work out," or "How can I help?" or "I'm sorry to hear that." Honestly, sometimes those words of "comfort" are actually a thinly-veiled way of dismissing what they're saying, but other times we are genuinely trying to ease their pain, lessen their burden, or soothe their worry.

Coaches don't seek to comfort. We are not therapists who use the power of conversation to bring healing. We are not parents who use words to soothe a child's pain. And we are not priests who speak words of comfort and absolution to sinners who have strayed and are in need solace. Nope. We are coaches. We use the power of conversation to promote growth, help people reach goals, and support client-generated solutions. Instead of trying to make things easy for the client, we push them to work harder, to think more deeply, and move beyond their comfort zone. We challenge our clients with the full expectation that the client will rise to the challenge and achieve something grand and/or become a stronger, more capable version of herself or himself.

Being a more challenging coach can be, well, challenging. I know it is for me. Recently I was talking with a capable and confident client who was preparing to have a series of one-on-one review sessions with her direct reports. Her strategy for conducting the review sessions seemed good. Her approach seemed *good*, but not *excellent*. I challenged her to improve her approach. I didn't know what improvements were needed; I wasn't even sure there was room for improvement. I just wanted to challenge her to do some exploring. Who knows, perhaps investing a few extra minutes thinking it through could bring much better results. I won't go into all the details here, but suffice it to say that within five minutes she upgraded her approach significantly by making two shifts. Pushing her to take the extra time, do the extra work, explore just a bit longer was not easy for either of us, but it was worth the discomfort.

The shift to being more challenging is not a shift everyone has to make. Some people are more than challenging: they push and prod in every single conversation they have ever had or ever will have. These people live at the far end of the spectrum in terms of making people feel uncomfortable. The technical term for these people is "jerk." When jerks are in a conversation, they never take into account the other person's feelings or situation. They just say whatever they want and very often their goal is to make the other person uncomfortable, prove the other person wrong, or somehow one-up the other person. This is obviously *not* the kind of challenge we strive for as coaches because this form of challenge is not client-centered. Jerks challenge for their own benefit, not to help anyone else. If you have jerk-like tendencies, then you'll need to re-orient your intentions and make a shift to a different kind of challenge in your conversations.

Fortunately, most people reading this book aren't jerks. Most of us have enough emotional intelligence to recognize what's happening with people in our conversations, and we adjust to keep them from feeling too pressed, cornered, convicted, or unsure. While this is very appropriate in everyday conversations, we may have to shift our conversational style to be professional-level coaches. As you make this shift, keep these things in mind:

- Keep the conversation safe. Challenging your clients does not mean judging, criticizing, or condemning. When a client feels unsafe, they shut down. A client who shuts down can't leverage their creativity and resourcefulness for their benefit.

- Invite the client to be the judge and jury. Don't challenge by being the one who determines the worth or value of the client's idea. As a coach, you're not in the position of expert. Instead, push the client to be the judge.
- Encourage the right way. When a client is challenged through the coaching conversation, he or she will need courage to rise up and face those challenges. An important coaching skill is the ability to encourage: literally to put courage into the other person. This doesn't mean you pump sunshine into them, slather false praise all over them, or act as their personal cheerleader. Instead, you should recognize their strengths, their successes, their progress, and their potential, and you should point these out to them.
- Keep the goodness of challenge in mind. When life is easy, people get bored. In contrast, people thrive most when facing challenging conditions. As the psychologist Mihaly Csikszentmihalyi has shown, when a person's level of skill is commensurate to the level of challenge they face, the person enters a state of "flow," which is a form of full engagement that is intrinsically rewarding. If you attempt to shield your client from challenge, you may prevent her from experiencing one of life's most rewarding circumstances: the opportunity to apply herself in a challenging situation.

So don't shy away from challenging your client. After all, he is already facing a challenge of some sort — this is why he hired you to coach him. You don't necessarily bring the challenge, you keep the challenge in front of him. We sometimes call this "holding the client's agenda." Even when they want to back away, get distracted, or take a big detour, we kindly invite them back to what they said they wanted to achieve in the conversation. Coaches are like the personal trainer who says, "You can only sit on the bike if you pedal it." We get our clients to work so they can achieve their ambitions, reach their goals, and transform their potential into reality.

Shift Five

Speak to Engage, Not to Control

O kay, so I admit that I may have left the toughest of the five shifts for last. This one is really tough. The language of coaching is spoken by persons who can engage in a conversation without trying to control. What do most people try to control? Two things.

First, we try to control the outcome of the conversation. When we try to control the outcome of the conversation, we may or may not be attempting to control the other person. We might not care about the other person all that much, but maybe we care about something in the conversation (*I must defend a person we're talking about or my position on the issue we're discussing*). Or perhaps we care about the length of the conversation (*I need to get out of this conversation ASAP*). Or maybe we just like to hear ourselves talk (*I need to get control of the conversation so I can pontificate on what I find interesting*). As ugly as it is to admit, most of us try to control the conversation so it meets our need, accomplishes our objective, or satisfies us in some way.

Second, we try to control the other person through the conversation. This second form of control has some overlap with the first one, but it is also distinct. While we probably wouldn't admit it, we use our words and the dialogue with other people in an effort to get them to do what we want them to do, what we'd like for them to believe, and/or what we think is best for them. As if our words were strings connected to a marionette, we maneuver the conversation to manipulate our conversation partner. I know that sounds harsh, but it's true. For some reason, we think we are really smart, extremely ethical, and that we see things far more clearly than anyone else. From this perspective, we try to control others with our words.

In coaching, this desire to control often presents itself in the coach trying to lead the client. When coaches lead, they (often subconsciously) race ahead of the client in forming an option, a solution, or an awareness. Then they try to steer the conversation and the client toward that option, solution, or awareness. When a coach is leading, it feels like they are helping — it feels this way to the coach and sometimes to the client as well. But while it might feel like helping, it's not. Coaches who lead their clients are actually mentoring, teaching, and consulting under the guise of coaching.

I've trained hundreds of coaches and the vast majority struggle with ceasing to lead the client. Sometimes they ask blatantly leading questions (*Don't you think you should talk to your boss first?*). Other times, they are subtler in their attempts to lead (*What permission do you need from your boss?*). I've even heard some beginner coaches say that coaching is a way of getting the client to do what the coach knows is best but to think that it's their (the client's) idea. I hesitate to deem this approach even "beginner" coaching because it's really not coaching at all.

Clients who are led may very well walk away with good options, solutions, and new awareness. However, their level of ownership is very low, which will eventually reveal itself in low motivation. In addition, by simply following the lead of the coach they have not strengthened their own capacity for expanding options, forming solutions, and generating new awareness.

The remedy for controlling is not to disengage. This is another common mistake beginner coaches sometimes make. They seem to think they should just sit back, relax, and listen to the client as if the client can figure things out just by hearing herself talk, talk, talk. While there is value in giving the client room to talk and plenty of space to explore, being disengaged is not a form of quality coaching. We need to disengage from our own agenda, but we need to be fully engaged with the client.

Fully engaged coaches are able to coach the person, not their problem. I wrote an entire eBook on this topic (*aptly titled Coach the Person Not the Problem*), so I won't go too deep into the issue here, but just know that when you coach the problem, you take responsibility for figuring things out and are much more likely to lead, control, and try to do the client's work for them. On the other hand, when you coach the person, you take responsibility for facilitating the client doing the work, figuring things out, and even recognizing how he or she needs to change in order to move forward.

SECTION THREE

Seven Language Elements
for Powerful Coaching

ow that you know the power of coaching and are (hopefully) developing fluency in the language of coaching, it's time to add some pizzazz to the mix. In this section we will explore what I call "language elements" — tools, techniques and best practices that will help you leverage the language of coaching for greater impact in your client relationships.

More than likely you're already employing some of these language elements. In those cases, let the chapter help move you toward eloquence and agility. Other language elements will be new to you. I'd encourage you to imagine how each of these elements might sound in your own coaching. What's a recent coaching conversation that could have been better with the use of this particular language element? When would you have used the element if only you had known about it?

Don't wait until you're perfectly confident and comfortable before you attempt to employ a language element. Learn the element, practice it in your head, and then once you feel slightly less than comfortable with the element, take the risk and go ahead and employ it in your actual coaching — after all, you'll never master these practices if you don't put them into practice.

Element One

The Power of Distinctions

Jill's relationship with her sister-in-law is not so hot. Jill finds her sister-in-law, Deb, to be aloof and kind of weird. Even Deb's young adult kids agree that Deb is hard to be around. In all, their relationship is somewhere between strained and estranged. But Deb's kids love Jill and Jill really wants to have a relationship with them. Jill also wants to support their relationship with Jill's kids and other cousins. But Jill faces a dilemma. She doesn't want to exclude Deb from the family dynamic, but she knows that Deb's presence at any family gatherings will lead others to be absent.

What should Jill do? What are her options for gathering the family and fostering healthy relationships while not unduly offending Deb?

This is a coaching circumstance where the power of distinctions can be leveraged, specifically the distinction between two extremes. For example, the coach might ask Jill to imagine a scenario in which the kids and other family members are fully considered with zero consideration given to Deb. The coach will have to invite Jill to envision how things would play out if she totally disregarded Deb. Next, the coach might ask Jill to imagine the opposite scenario: one in which Deb is fully considered and Jill does everything possible to include Deb and avoid offending her, even at the expense of Jill's interest in fostering great relationships among the other family members. These two scenarios will stand in stark contrast to one another and the contrast will very likely highlight some new awareness of intuitive insight for Jill.

The coach might even go so far as to ask Jill to pick one word or phrase to describe the first scenario and a different word to represent the second one. Perhaps Jill chooses "screw Deb!" for the first one and "bend over backwards" for the second. These two phrases allow Jill to quickly and succinctly consider the options and recognize the contrast. Who knows where such a conversation might go, but one possibility is that Jill could question her belief that leaving Deb out is tantamount to "screw Deb!" She might choose to reframe that option in a way that is less about Deb and more about the family. Again, we don't know (nor do we attempt to plan ahead) what a distinction might generate for the client.

The conversation with Jill is an example of one type of distinction (extremes) that coaches can employ. Here are some others:

- **Best Case vs. Worst Case Scenario**. This is another type of extreme, but specifically best and worst. I typically find this type of distinction helpful when a client is considering doing something or not doing it, as opposed to deciding between two or more options.

- **Current vs. Future State**. A very common tactic in coaching involves asking the client to envision how their preferred future state is distinct from their current state. The coach can invite the client to make these distinctions by formulating narrative and descriptive sentences, or by using key words, images, or metaphors.

- **Needs vs. Wants**. As difficult as it is for each of us to admit, our needs and our wants are not the same thing. Helping a client make a distinction between what they want (prefer) from a situation and what they need (must have) can often bring things into clearer focus.

- **Selfish vs. Self-care**. When a client is struggling to set and enforce boundaries, make requests, or in some other way take care of self at the possible expense of another's preferences, they can find it hard to distinguish between being selfish and practicing self-care. Simply asking the client how they'd know the difference can create powerful new awareness.

- **Control vs. Influence vs. Concern**. As Stephen Covey pointed out so well in *The 7 Habits of Highly Effective People*, there are many things about which we have concern, but much less over which we have influence. He encouraged readers to focus on where they have influence. Sometimes I like to go even further and ask the client to distinguish where they have influence from where they have control. A parent might have influence over their teenage child, but they have very little control. Making the distinction can help the parent navigate the relationship much more effectively.

- **Perfect vs. Good Enough**. Some clients find it challenging to know how well to perform a task, what to expect from a relationship, and/ or what to expect from themselves. Some clients struggle with perfectionism. Others are far too willing to settle short. The distinction between perfect and good enough can give the perfectionist permission to ratchet down their expectations by establishing standards that are good enough (perhaps even "excellent") without being perfect. Meanwhile, I've also seen this distinction prompt the settler to step things up by removing the concern that "good enough" will necessarily mean doing things perfectly (a standard they know they cannot meet).

- **Something I Could Do vs. Something I Will Do**. When a client explores options for addressing a concern or opportunity, they often find one or more very workable solutions. Sometimes they'll even phrase the option as "I could…." Paying close attention to their language, the coach will notice that such a phase means the client is considering an option, not committing to it. Just because it's a good option doesn't mean the client will do it or even wants to do it. Drawing out the distinction between what the client *could do* versus what the client *will do* helps pinpoint commitment and motivation, both of which are necessary for real change.

- **Interests vs. Positions**. This is one of the most important distinctions to make, especially when dealing with couples, teams, or groups that might be experiencing conflict or competing ideas. This is a distinction that the coach might have to explain a bit in order for it to have impact. As Roger Schwarz points out in *The Skilled Facilitator*, an interest is what a person truly wants from a solution while a position is the means for getting what they want. For example, a client might be considering going back to school, but his spouse is opposed because of the costs. The disagreement is severe at the position level since "go to school" and "not go to school" are incompatible. But there could be many ways forward at the interests level. For example, perhaps the client wants to learn new skills that will help him further his career while his spouse wants to avoid going in debt. Those two interests are not incompatible, though it might take some creativity and collaboration to find a way forward that meets both of their interests.

- **Imperfect vs. Toxic.** I have a client who is committed to getting the very best from each of her direct reports. She is flexible, responsible, and competent. However, recently she described one direct report who just seems impervious to even great management. My client fully "owned" the situation and wanted to explore options for adjusting her management style to unlock the employee's potential. After some discussion, I asked her to consider the difference between a normally imperfect person (after all, every person is imperfect in some ways) and a toxic person. I shared with her some of the common traits of a toxic personality: manipulative, judgmental, doesn't take responsibility for their own feelings, make you prove yourself to them, etc. The distinction helped my client identify the employee as someone who was not likely to respond well to even the very best management tactics. All clients must adjust to the everyday imperfections of other people, but no client should attempt to accommodate to a toxic personality.

- **Puzzle vs. Problem vs. Dilemma vs. Mystery.** In their helpful book *coachbook: A Guide to Organizational Coaching Strategies and Practices*, the authors describe four distinct types of issues leaders face. A puzzle is one-dimensional and has an answer. A problem is a bit more complex, involves more than one perspective and needs a solution (not an answer). A dilemma is much more complex, involves two valid polarities, and it can be managed but never really solved. Finally, a mystery is unfathomable, unpredictable and the leader simply has to learn to live with it. Distinguishing these types of issues can help the client avoid applying overly simplistic or complex approaches. For example, I've coached many business owners who've generated great success by answering puzzles and solving problems, but who get flummoxed when they encounter a dilemma or, heaven forbid, a mystery. Once they see the distinctions, they learn to spot dilemmas and mysteries and to respond to them appropriately instead of spinning their wheels looking for a solution.

As you can see, distinctions come in many flavors and can be applied to address a wide variety of coaching situations. When should we employ distinctions? Here are times when distinctions might be helpful:

- When a client is stuck in the same (perhaps negative) use of language.
- When a client could benefit from being introduced to a new and similar concept.
- When a client brings up a distinction (perhaps unknowingly).
- When there is lack of clarity or lack of commitment.

Finally, consider these tips for using distinctions effectively:

- Use the client's words, when possible. If the client is concerned about being self-centered, draw out a distinction between self-centered and self-care instead of trying to get them to use the word *selfish*.
- Ask the client to make meaning, define differences, and create contrast. When the client does the work, they tend to get the value. Don't do too much of the work for them.
- Get permission to share what you see. When you do see something they might be missing, quickly ask permission before sharing. But beware: just because the client grants permission doesn't mean the client is agreeing to agree with what you share before you share it.

- Bring up distinctions later in the session or even later in the coaching relationship. Let things develop and allow the client time to experience what they are experiencing before jumping in too quickly with a distinction.
- Support the client in holding onto the awareness that comes from distinctions. The key is not for the client to remember the distinction, per se, but instead to remember the new awareness that the distinction generated and to then apply it in actions that supports the client's agenda.

Element Two

Synthesis

If you asked a beginner coach what a great coach does really well, the beginner coach will likely respond with "Ask great questions." But if you ask a seasoned coach what a great coach does really well, they will very likely respond with "Listen well." Asking and listening are the twin, interrelated skills that a coach must master, and both are incredibly important. However, while powerful questions get much of the focus and attention, listening is often underrated. It's been said that in the game of golf "you drive for show and putt for dough." Applying that mantra to coaching, we can say that questions are impressive, but listening is what really distinguishes great coaching from mediocre coaching.

Synthesizing is an advanced aspect of listening that can really improve your coaching game. In our book *Coaching for Christian Leaders,* my friend and co-author Linda Miller emphasizes the importance of synthesizing: "This is a critical skill in coaching, because coaching conversations go in so many directions. Coaches who synthesize are able to track themes from different conversations (or even in the same conversation) and link them together."

Synthesizing should not be confused with summarizing or rephrasing what you've heard from your coaching client. Those are helpful and important aspects of listening, too. However, synthesizing goes beyond these forms of active listening in that the coach who synthesizes is listening not only to what is being shared and what has been shared, but also notices how various aspects of what the client says fit together into a bigger picture.

Synthesizing can involve seeing a bigger picture, noticing broad patterns and themes, or recognizing how seemingly different issues are connected. For example, I recently talked with a client who was frustrated with a request a family member had made of her. The family member asked my client for some free professional help (my client is an attorney). My client willingly provided the help, which took a couple of hours and which also left her feeling frustrated. She wasn't sure why her frustration was so great. I recalled that in a previous session she'd mentioned not having time to buy groceries that week, and I asked her if maybe the two were connected. She blurted out, "Yes! I am pulled in so many directions that it felt just plain rude for my family member to assume I had an extra two or three hours to work on their question." This allowed the conversation to turn from the issue of frustration to the deeper issues of allowing herself to be overwhelmed, not standing up for herself, and (eventually) sabotaging her own wellbeing. By synthesizing, I invited the client to the new awareness that it wasn't her family member who was being rude, but my client was being rude to herself by agreeing to help.

Synthesizing is an effective way to help our clients notice what's going on from a fresh perspective. One of the major outcomes we expect from a coaching session is new awareness for the client, and synthesizing is totally aimed at spurring the client to see a new internal or situational awareness.

Synthesize – don't diagnose. Seeing a connection is not the same thing as seeing a reason or spotting a root cause. And since coaches are not in the business of diagnosing, prescribing, or curing, we shouldn't employ our listening skills toward such aims. Also, be open to the fact that some of the connections you think you see are not in fact real for the client. When you offer a possible connection, a pattern, or a theme, the client might not see it, might not agree with it, or might not see it yet. That's okay – just move on.

If you want to improve your ability to synthesize, try these suggestions:

- Take notes. Keep your notes simple and brief (don't try to capture everything) and review them often. Reviewing notes from previous sessions can help you notice connections in today's session.
- Know your preference for details vs. big picture. Synthesis requires the coach to notice details and to connect details into a bigger pic-

ture, and most people have a preference for one or the other. In MBTI terms, Intuitives prefer the big picture and Sensors prefer the details. Knowing which you prefer can help you be more intentional with the other.

- Ask the client to notice themes and patterns and to make connections. Many clients can do this when invited to do so. When a coach asks, "What's a theme in your work?" or "How does this issue fit any kind of pattern in your life?" the client can essentially teach the coach how to synthesize.

- Work with an advanced coach and notice how he or she does it. Working with a coach not only allows you to deal with your own issues and opportunities, but it's also a great way to increase your coaching ability.

Element Three

Formulas

As you master the language of coaching, you'll find times when it's best to take a powerful but complex idea and boil it down, simplify it, and make it more accessible. One way to do this is through the use of a formula. In coaching, a formula is like a recipe or equation that packages an idea to make it more useful to the client.

One of my favorite formulas comes from Timothy Gallwey's book *The Inner Game of Work*. Gallwey got his start as a tennis coach, then golf, then applied what he learned from sports to the world outside of sports. In order to develop a person's latent capability, it's helpful to use the formula $P = p - i$, or Performance = potential - interference. In this equation, Performance (P) in any activity, from hitting a ball to solving a complex leadership issue, is equal to one's potential (p) after the interference (i) has been subtracted. As Gallwey notes from his career as a sports and corporate coach, "Performance rarely equals potential. A little self-doubt, an erroneous assumption, the fear of failure, was all it took to greatly diminish one's performance." (17)

Using Gallwey's formula can help a client explore what's possible (potential) and find motivation there. The client can scrutinize their own performance and notice what's good and what's not so good. They can also note the distinction between performance and potential. And much new awareness comes when the client examines the interferences that are preventing their potential from being fully expressed. Recognizing and reducing the interference is the eventual goal when using this formula.

I often use the performance formula to help a team process their performance in a way that keeps all team members on the same page. For example, when working with a church leadership team, I broke the large team into three small groups. One small group brainstormed ideas describing the team's current performance (what's the current reality). A second small group addressed the team's potential (what's possible for this team). A third small group addressed the interferences that were holding the team back. The groups rotated twice so that each small group addressed all three of the factors before reconvening and sharing in the large group. After hearing and sharing, I coached the team to identify three key actions that could improve performance.

Another formula I sometimes use is expressed as X to Y by Z. This is a simple coaching formula that lets the client describe where they are (X), where they'd like to be (Y) and the time and effort it will take to close the gap (Z). The formula comes from Stephen Covey's book *The Four Disciplines of Execution: Achieving Your Wildly Important Goals* in which it's described as a formula for setting goals. While Covey's version assigns only the value of time to Z (by when), I have found that my coaching clients get more value from the formula when Z represent the time *and* effort it will take to close the gap. This slight variation turns it from a goal-setting formula to a coaching tool that clarifies the important aspects of creating change in one's life or work.

Coaches can collect formulas related to issues their clients face and then bring those formulas into the coaching when the time is right. We can also allow a formula to emerge, on the spot, within a coaching conversation. In fact, you can even request that a client express an important truth in a formula format.

How to use formulas:

- Make the formula brief and memorable. Your clients will not find it helpful should you employ a formula with twenty-seven variables and a logarithm.
- Use the client's words, if possible. You can even edit how you express a favorite formula by using the client's words. If you usually talk about $P = p - i$, but your client is talking about "success" instead of performance, you could swap out success for performance resulting in the formula $S = p - i$.

- Explore all variables. A formula brings together several aspects of an issue, each of which is important. Don't focus on just one aspect. Instead, explore all of them to some degree, taking a deeper dive into the ones that need more attention.
- Don't overdo it! Part of what makes formulas so powerful is that they are not used all that often. Your client will not find it helpful should you have a different formula for practically every issue the client faces. Being fluent in a language requires you employ language elements selectively, at the right time.

Finally, when should you use a formula? Some occasions are more ripe for formulas than others. Here are some of the reasons you might chose to use a formula:

- To clarify the path from one point to another.
- To provide an easily remembered equation for success.
- To help your client visualize the steps involved in solving a problem.
- To provide a simple focusing tool to guide conversation.
- To break down a complex issue into simpler components.

Element Four

Story-telling

Stories have proven to be one of the most powerful and long-lasting tools of human language, no matter the language. People love stories because they convey practical wisdom and stimulate new awareness. Long before people were able to write things down, we held onto important truths by embedding them into memorable stories such as fables, myths, fairy tales, and proverbs.

Coaches can use stories to help promote discovery for our clients. To do so, we need to be good at story-telling and we need to have a reservoir of relevant stories. Our stories can come from the classics such as Aesop's fables or Christian scripture. We can also share stories of fact, such as episodes from history or the news.

One of my clients – I'll call him Tom – was a such a successful business owner that it seemed he was unable to do anything but succeed in business. On the other hand, Tom's family life left a lot to be desired. He was miserable. His children were turning into characters nobody wanted to be around, including Tom and his wife. The relationship between Tom and his wife was becoming colder and more distant by the month. While he had many business associates, he had only a few friends, and none of them could be described as close. Tom was frustrated that his success and wealth was not generating the good life he desired. "In fact," he declared, "it seems like my business success is the source of my relationship woes."

This was a great opportunity to remind Tom of the story of King Midas. To be honest, this story is almost too familiar to be used effectively in coaching, but I thought I'd give it a try. "What you're going through reminds me of an old Greek legend. Dionysus was a god whose adopted dad went missing. So Dionysus issued a kind of ancient Silver Alert. When a human king found the old man, he treated him well and returned him to Dionysus, who was so grateful he offered the king a reward of whatever he wanted. The king thought about it and asked that whatever he touched would turn to gold. In one version of the story, Midas died of starvation because it's hard to eat an apple of gold. In another version, he reached out to comfort his daughter only to have her turn to gold, so he begged Dionysus to remove the 'gift.' Dionysus told Midas to wash in a nearby river to remove the power and that whatever he placed in the river would be reversed of the golden touch. Tom, it seems that you have the Midas touch and it's up to you to decide which version of the story you'll live out."

The story made Tom uncomfortable. He pushed back: "I don't think life's an either/or. I think I can be successful and have a good family and friends." I replied, "Maybe so. That hasn't been your story so far. What do you think the lesson of Midas is?" He thought about it before responding, "Be careful what you wish for. You might get what you think you want, but at the cost of what really matters." I asked, "So what really matters to you?" He quickly declared that his family was what really mattered to him. Without a word from me, he followed up by confessing, "I don't act like it. My business is so successful not because I have a golden touch, but because I give it my best. If I gave my family my best, I think things would be different." I asked in what ways things would be different. "My family life would be stronger, closer, happier. But my business might be less successful." What emerged was a tender moment, into which I asked, "If having a stronger, closer, happier family required you to be cleansed of your gift for business success, would you wash in the river?" "I would," he declared. "What would that look like?" And with that question, Tom was on the path to radically re-orienting his life according to what he truly valued.

When telling a story, coaches want the keep the client interested. This is why I waited before revealing that the king was Midas. I didn't want my client to run too far ahead in his own mind and lose the power of the story. We also want to include enough detail to make it a story, but not so many details that the client gets lost or wonders where this is going. You can adjust the length and nature of the story to fit your client's personality.

When telling a story, you'll also want to keep these other principles in mind:

- Be brief. If you look at <u>Aesop's fables</u>, you'll be amazed at the economy of language used. Stories that have stood the test of time are incredibly short. Aim for telling a story in less than two minutes.

- Keep it relevant. Sometimes a story seems relevant in your mind, but the connection isn't clear to your client. If it's not fairly obvious how the story connects with what your client is facing, the story is probably not a great fit. You don't want to spend more time explaining the connection than sharing the story.

- Let the point/lesson be discovered by the client. Great stories have built-in meaning, but the exact interpretation of that meaning is somewhat dependent on the person hearing the story. Remain open and flexible to what meaning your client draws and resist using storytelling as a way to get your point across. When I shared about King Midas, I wasn't sure exactly what the client would take from the ancient talke, I just knew my client's circumstance was similar to that of Midas.

- Ask for reflection/application to the client's situation. The moral of the story isn't nearly as important as the application of the moral in the client's life. All good coaching sessions result in new awareness and new action, so make sure you invite the client to articulate not only what she is taking away from the story, but also what she's going to do as a result.

Element Five

Models

The language of coaching is most powerfully experienced when the conversation displays a dynamic tension between order and chaos. The conversation has to be free to expand and unfold in unexpected ways (chaos) if there is to be discovery. On the other hand, structure often prompts discovery while also providing a channel for new awareness to flow toward powerful results-producing action. One of the ways the coach can bring stimulating structure to the coaching relationship is through the use of models.

A model is a simplified representation of reality. For example, if you're going to navigate the reality of New York City's subway, a map that simplifies the large and complex subway system will come in handy. Likewise, in the world of coaching, a model helps you better understand and navigate reality. By seeing the model, you can better comprehend the real thing.

In coaching, a model represents some larger truth that is helpful to the coach, to the client, or to both. There are three basic types of models.

First, there are **Conversation Models**. A coaching conversation model represents an entire coaching conversation, usually from beginning to end, noting the order and flow of the conversation. For example, one of the most popular coaching models is the *GROW Model* that was propagated by Sir John Whitmore in his book *Coaching for Performance*. The GROW Model provides a structure for a given coaching conversation: start by clarifying the client's Goals, then move to describing the Reality of the situation, next look at Options that could close the gap between reality and goal, and finally explore the client's Will to take action on one of the options.

Another conversation model we teach at Coach Approach Ministries is the **Hourglass Model**, which was developed by one of our founders, Jane Creswell, MCC. The Hourglass Model uses the metaphor of an hourglass to represent three distinct phases of a coaching conversation. The top of the hourglass begins wide (What do you want to talk about?), explores the issue broadly, and narrows the topic to a point of focus as the conversation narrows toward the neck of the hourglass. The neck of the hourglass is a nice representation of the "pinch point" for the client. For example, if the client's topic is time management, the coach might help her discover that the pinch point is how to deal with interruptions, especially since her company pushes an "open door policy" for all managers. Once the focus is discovered, the conversation ceases to narrow and starts expanding to explore options, possibilities, and what if's. The bottom half of the hourglass can involve dreaming, brainstorming, and anything else that stirs the client's creativity and resourcefulness for coming up with possible paths forward. Finally, as the sand piles up and forms a mini mountain in the bottom half of the hourglass, the coach invites the client to narrow the options, to identify the best one(s) and to design those actions into real-world actions. In the same way that the top of the sand pile aligns with the narrow neck of the hourglass, the client's best actions must align with the pinch point of the topic. In other words, their actions need to actually address the heart of the matter for this topic. (By clicking the link at the end of this eBook you can get a free PDF of The Hourglass Model.)

When using a conversation model, feel free to share the model with the client. Sharing the model can help the client know how to be coached since the client will know where the two of you are in the conversation. The model can also help you and the client create the awareness that is needed at the moment. For example, instead of rushing ahead to explore options early in the conversation, a model will help you know that options come later, after you've explored the issue a bit. Conversation models can also be helpful for new coaches who struggle to know what to ask next. The model keeps the coach from getting lost in the conversation.

While conversation models can be very useful, they can also be problematic. Remember, models represent reality, but not perfectly. No coaching conversation follows a model perfectly and precisely. The structure offered by the model can squeeze the life right out of the model if the coach leans too heavily on the model and tries to force the conversation to conform flawlessly to the model.

Second, coaches use **Awareness Models**. These models represent a truth that might help the client better understand and address his coaching issue. You can think of these as "teaching lessons" that the client can apply to his situation. While the coach is not an instructor who offers solutions, it's perfectly fine for a coach to bring in a model that might support the client in better understanding his situation.

One popular and simple awareness model comes from Stephen Covey's *7 Habits of Highly Effective People*. In this classic book and workshop, Covey describes **The Circle of Concern vs. Circle of Influence**. You've probably seen this model, which represents one's circle of influence (matters over which a person actually has influence) as a small circle within the much larger circle of concern (matters about which a person is concerned). The truth conveyed by the model is that most of what concerns us we can do little or nothing about (the weather, the economy, gossip at work, how other people choose to respond, my past behaviors, etc.), but there are areas of life where we have great influence (how I dress, what I eat, what I say, how I respond, etc.). The model reminds clients that they cannot change other people — they can only deal with their own stuff.

Another awareness model I sometimes use with clients is the **Strengths vs. Skills Model**, which was also developed by my friend Jane Creswell. The model actually predates the StrengthsFinder movement and assessment, so don't confuse the two. Jane represents one's natural strengths as the foundation of a building and one's skills as bricks that build upon the foundation. The foundation is unchanging and innate, while the learned competencies develop throughout life. I won't go into the details of the model in this book (use the link at the end of the book to access a short video in which I teach the model), but one of the main lessons from the model is that problems arise when we add skills that are unsupported by our strengths. I use the model when a client finds himself in a role that he can do (he's developed the skills for it), but which is not really a fit for him (usually he feels like a fraud or is super stressed by the challenges of the role).

Another awareness model I use is the **Transition Model** that William Bridges details in his book *Managing Transitions*. A transition is the psychological process by which a person deals with significant change. It's the inner process by which a person's insides (attitudes, feeling, thoughts, etc.) catch up with the changes that are happening on the outside. The model illustrates the three stages of a transition and where a person's energy gets focused in each stage. It's an incredibly helpful model for aiding clients who are in the midst of transition because it helps them frame their experience and recognize what they need most in the moment. I've also found it to be a good model to share with leaders who are implementing change initiatives without taking into account the stress the experience will generate for others. As Bridges says, change is hard, but it's the transitions that will do you in.

Awareness models are great for fostering new learning for your clients. When you coach within a niche, you'll almost accidentally develop a repertoire of models that will be useful in coaching. There are awareness models for time management, relationships, developing routines, changing habits, managing people, finding a career fit, etc. So when you come across a great model, study it, use it, and master it to the point that you can teach it quickly, simply, and powerfully.

When using awareness models, keep these principles in mind:

- Make sure the model fits the moment. Clients who are confused as to why you're sharing a model will get little value from your awesome model, so make sure to connect the model to the issue before sharing the model.
- Share the model quickly. Aim to take no more than 5 minutes for a more complex model like the Strengths vs. Skills Model. For a simpler model such as the Circle of Concern vs. Circle of Influence, keep it to a minute or less.
- Let the model teach the truth. If it's a good model, the client will see how it relates to his own situation. If you have to spell everything out for the client, you're probably doing too much work and maybe the model doesn't fit as well as you thought it would.

- Turn things over to the client. Share the model, then transition the conversation back to the client and the client's issue. You can do this by asking something along the lines of, "What connection do you see for your situation?"

Finally, coaches also use **Behind-the-Scenes Models**. Each of these models represents a truth that informs the way the coach believes the world works and therefore shapes the coach's interaction with the client. I refer to these models as "behind-the-scenes" because they are used implicitly by the coach. Such models rarely come forward into the shared space between coach and client in an explicit way. Instead, these models work in the background by informing the kinds of questions, exercises and other techniques the coach uses.

One example of a behind-the-scenes model in my own coaching is the **Jungian personality type theory**. While I happen to be certified to administer the Myers-Briggs Type Indicator, even when I don't ask the client to complete the MBTI, the framework still informs my coaching. This theory of personality holds that each person displays some degree of preference in four areas: expression (introversion/extraversion), perceiving (sensing/intuition), judging (thinking/feeling), and lifestyle (judging/perceiving). When the four preferences combine, the person displays one of sixteen personality types. I rarely go into all the juicy details of a client's personality preferences in the coaching conversation. Instead, I let the model inform my coaching in two ways.

First, when I know the client's type, I adapt my coaching according to her preferences. For example, a client who prefers intuition will tend to trust patterns, theories, themes, and what can appear to be hunches (vs. a sensing person who prefer information that is tangible, present and concrete). Since an intuitive person is more comfortable processing possibilities, I tend to invite her to explore her topic by peering into the future and dreaming of what might be. One the other hand, I tend to invite Sensors to conduct their initial exploration of a topic by noticing the details of the issue before asking them to move into setting goals.

This isn't the place for us to go super deep into how to use MBTI in coaching, but I should point out that I don't always try to tap into the client's preferred way of operating. For example, I might intentionally go against the grain by asking an extraverted client to take a moment of silence to ponder before responding or by assigning homework that is reflective instead of active. Just because a client has a preference for extraversion over introversion doesn't mean the client cannot or should not act in inward-focused ways.

The second way I let the MBTI model inform my coaching is to apply it more generally, apart from a client's specific preferences or type. Jungian personality theory provides me a framework — a way of looking at the world that informs how I interact with other people, including those whom I coach. For example, people process decisions based on a thinking function (in an objective way using logic, causality and reason) and a feeling function (in a subjective way using empathy, considering harmony and relationships). Knowing this allows me to ask questions that engage both functions. While a client's particular preference may determine which decision-making function he will trust more, I don't need to know his preference to know that it's a good idea to ask questions based on both functions.

Okay, that's probably enough about MBTI. (You have to watch out for MBTI folks — we will geek out on the topic of personality types all day long!) What about some other examples? Where do coaches find other behind-the-scenes models? One place to look is at other assessment tools, many of which can provide a framework to inform your coaching. Here are two examples from my own coaching experience:

- **Conflict Styles**. The Thomas-Kilmann Conflict Mode Instrument describes five basic ways of interacting with others in conflict situations (that is, times when the concerns of two people appear to be incompatible). Knowing these five ways helps me invite clients to explore the best way to show up in times of conflict.
- **Relational Orientation**. The Fundamental Interpersonal Relations Orientation (FIRO) describes three sets of relationship behaviors: control, inclusion, and affection. For each area, a person has certain needs for *expressing* behaviors and certain needs for *wanting* others to express behaviors. For example, a person with a high expression need in affection will tend to initiate affectionate behaviors. They will be

the first to give a hug, say nice things, and show support for others. A person with a high wanting need in affection will tend to be receptive and even desirous of affectionate behavior from others while a person with a low wanting need in affection will prefer you keep those hugs to yourself. Knowing about these three areas (affection, control, inclusion) and the two types of behavior (expressing and wanting) informs my coaching as I support clients who are navigating relationships at work or at home.

Assessment tools aren't the only place to look for behind-the-scenes models. Theories of human development, organizational development, moral development, change, and leadership can also provide helpful frameworks for coaches. This is why coaches need to be well-read, especially in areas of their coaching niche. For example, if you coach leaders, you probably want to have some leadership models that inform your coaching. Ken Blanchard's *Situational Leadership II* could be helpful, as would the five practices of exemplary leadership as described in Kouzes and Posner's book *The Leadership Challenge.*

You can even develop your own behind-the-scenes model based on what you've learned about how humans work. After a lot of research in the areas of change, growth, and transformation as well as years of coaching experience, I developed a model that frames three levels of change. I call this the Deep Change Model. (Use the link at the end of the book to receive a one-page PDF of this model)

Element Six

Metaphors

Coaches are communicators. We specialize in effective communication in order to draw out what's inside our client's head, straighten out their tangled thought noodles, and clarify the fuzzy pictures of what's possible. And one of the most effective ways to communicate well is the use of metaphors. A metaphor is a figure of speech that describes an object or action in a way that is not literally true but helps explain an idea or makes a comparison. As a coach, you don't literally draw out what's inside your client's head – that would be creepy and illegal. And your client's thoughts are not literally noodles or overly pixelated pictures. While metaphors are not literally true, the use of them in our communication is powerful. In coaching, metaphors work for three reasons.

First, metaphors can simplify complex ideas. My friend and coaching colleague Bill Copper is fond of using a metaphor to describe how coaching works by creating ownership with the client. He says, "Nobody washes a rental car." The picture of refusing the car wash when fueling up your rental car before turning it in at the airport is simple, easy to understand, and gets you thinking. On the other hand, the reasons why coaching clients are motivated and accountable for the ideas they generate (versus the ideas handed to them by someone else) is kind of complicated. While it's not rocket science, it is brain science. We could unpack all the reasons behind this truth and explain it with long, descriptive paragraphs, but doing so would take a lot of time and would be easy to misunderstand. It's easy to get lost in long, complicated, and complex descriptions. It's not easy to get lost in a metaphor. Come to think of it, "getting lost" is another metaphor. They're everywhere!

Second, metaphors can familiarize the unknown. Some things are tough to understand not because they are complicated, but because they are unknown to us. When a client moves forward in life, her progress is going to take her into unfamiliar territory, and a metaphor can shed light on the unknown.

For example, I once had a client who was a business owner who succeeded at every step – until he didn't. When his business took a very hard hit, he had no idea how to respond. While he was familiar with the challenges that accompany growth, he was a stranger to the challenges that come from losing business. The client was also an amateur pilot, so we compared his business circumstances to a plane that was plummeting towards the earth. The Denzel Washington movie *Flight* had recently come out, so that helped with the metaphor. I asked him what he'd do if his plane took a nosedive. Honestly, his response included some aeronautical terminology that I didn't really understand – something about speed, lift, and gravity. The comparison helped him realize that businesses also faced a type of gravity that constantly and naturally pulls them down. The force of gravity is strong, but it can be overcome with the right design, enough speed, and a well-trained pilot. Eventually he said that the worst thing a pilot can do is freak out. Then, after a long pause, he admitted that he was kind of freaking out. That confession turned the focus of the conversation to how he could stay calm in order to be the best leader possible. The familiar concept tapped into his resources, which he then leveraged to deal with an unknown reality. That's the power of metaphors in coaching.

Third, metaphors can reduce fear. When a person faces complicated and/or unknown circumstances, the natural response is fear. This emotional reaction is designed to keep humans alive by encouraging us to avoid potentially dangerous situations. But avoiding scary stuff is not always an option. What's worse, when gripped by a negative emotion such as fear, the human brain goes into shut down mode. The body's fight-or-flight response pumps blood (and the oxygen it carries) to our big muscles so we can run or struggle, but this reallocation of blood also depletes the brain of the oxygen it needs to be creative and resourceful. In other words, fear makes us dumb. By simplifying the complex and familiarizing the unknown, metaphors reduce fear and increase the brain's ability to function at full capacity.

Given the power of metaphors to serve our coaching clients, we should seek to use them well. If metaphors don't come naturally for you, here are some simple hints as to where to find good ones and how to use them well:

- Don't miss the metaphors your client is already using. I once observed a coaching session when the client said he felt caught between first base and second base, unsure which way to go. The coach didn't catch the metaphor and it took another ten minutes for the coach to recognize the pickle the client was facing.

- Tap into your client's hobbies and interests. During the intake session and throughout the coaching relationship, you will find out all kinds of neat things about your client that can inform the metaphors you employ. For example, if your client plays golf, you've got a lot of options for employing golf metaphors at some point in the coaching relationship.

- Don't overdo it. By the sixteenth golf metaphor your client is going to regret having ever mentioned his hobby. He might even get teed off, so don't use the same source for all your metaphors. And don't stretch the metaphor too far. Every metaphor breaks down eventually.

- Don't confuse a metaphor with an allegory. I don't mean to bring back harsh flashbacks of high school English class, but a metaphor (a simple comparison) is not the same things as an allegory (a complex comparison where each element in the word picture represents something or someone in reality). If I'd used an allegory with my amateur pilot business client, then we would have looked for a corresponding reality for every aspect of flight. In coaching, allegories tend to make things more complicated as you attempt to fit reality into the word picture. My advice is to avoid allegories.

Take a look at your own use of metaphors. How are you doing? To what extent do metaphors come naturally to you? Think back to a recent coaching conversation and consider what metaphors might have been helpful. If you'd like some immediate application, try coming up with a metaphor to describe your use of metaphors. As you grow in your ability to use metaphors well, your coaching will take off and soar.

Element Seven

Sharing Self

New coaches have to make the shift to believing that expertise resides in the client. This can be tough for new coaches. After all, most of us believe that we help others most by offering our own brilliant insights and awesome advice. So when you're new to coaching, it's helpful to resist sharing your own stuff. By resisting the urge to bring your own story into the coaching, you build the capacity to rely on the client's creativity, resourcefulness, and expertise. However, once you learn how to treat the client as the expert, you can exercise a bit more freedom to share self. Using the skills of sharing self involves knowing when (and when not) to share, as well as how to share.

To share self is to bring your own experience into the coaching relationship on behalf of the client. Let's be clear, the coach does not share to make the coach seem like the hero or the smart person in the coaching relationship. You have to keep the conversation focused on the client and the client's agenda, but there are times when it's helpful to bring some of the coach's story into the relationship.

What kinds of things can the coach share? For starters, it might be helpful to share:

- An experience you had that is similar to the client's current experience to encourage the client. Sometimes a client can feel like she is the only one going through a particular challenge. In those times, knowing you're not alone can reduce the stress and breathe hope into the situation.

- Some subject-matter knowledge you acquired that is relevant to the client's situation.
- A different perspective.

We share self only when sharing is obviously relevant to what the client is talking about. Going off topic or pursuing a tangent with our story is not only distracting, but doing so can also diminish trust and shift the dynamic of the coaching relationship in a negative way.

Sharing self typically occurs in three stages. First, you recognize an opportunity when sharing will benefit the client. Next, you do the sharing. The key is to keep things brief and relevant. You're not a raconteur who tells a long and winding story that confuses the client until finally revealing a powerful truth at the very end of the story. That's not coaching. Keep things concise and share in a way that makes it obvious that you're doing so for the benefit of the client. Finally, transition back to the client, allowing her to "own" what you just shared to whatever extent she chooses. Keep the emphasis on the client's application of what you shared, not on the details of your story or your experience. Remember, you share self as a way of keeping the spotlight of the conversation on the client not to shift the spotlight to yourself.

Conclusion

My goal in writing this short eBook was to help you develop your ability to speak the language of coaching with fluency and for greater impact. Effective coaching creates two results for the person being coached: new awareness and new actions. No book can replace the power of a coaching relationship, but hopefully this book generated those same results for you.

Before closing the book, take a few minutes to consider the new awareness you've received:

1. If you can only retain one or two lessons from this book, what do you want to make sure you carry forward?
2. What will it look like for you to integrate your new learning into your coaching?
3. Where can you start applying what you've learned?
4. In addition to any "head knowledge" you gained from this book, what encouragement or motivation did you receive?
5. What do you hope will be different in your coaching as a result of what you gained from this book?
6. Finally, what do you hope will be different in the world as a result of your improved coaching?

That final question is the big one. As coaches, we change the world through the people we coach. What you do is important.

In the Hebrew scripture we read that God created the world by speaking it into existence. In a similar manner, you and those you coach will spark powerful creativity through your coaching conversations. Keep this powerful truth in mind as you continue to develop your ability to speak the language of coaching.

Free Resources

Go to www.coachapproachministries.org/language to get free access to the resources mentioned in the book, including:

- A video teaching of the Strengths vs. Skills Model
- An infographic of the Hourglass Model
- A one-page description of the Deep Change Model

Other Books from Coach Approach Ministries

- *The Coaching Mindset: 8 Ways to Think Like a Coach*
- *Coach the Person, Not the Problem: A Simple Guide to Coaching for Transformation*
- *Faith Coaching: A Conversational Approach to Helping Others Move Forward in Faith*
- *Coaching for Christian Leaders: A Practical Guide*